Daily Life

The Gold Rush

Stuart A. Kallen
P. M. Boekhoff

KidHaven Press

KidHaven Press, an imprint of Gale Group, Inc.
10911 Technology Place, San Diego, CA 92127

Cover: Gold diggers, North America, 1849.

Library of Congress Cataloging-in-Publication Data

Boekhoff, P. M. (Patti Marlene), 1957–
The Gold Rush / by P.M. Boekhoff and Stuart A. Kallen.
p. cm. — (Daily Life)
Includes bibliographical references and index.
Summary: Discusses the California gold rush including the discovery of gold at Sutter's Mill in 1848, the migration of people to California, life in California's mining camps and boom towns, and the crime, racism, and frontier justice that followed.
ISBN 0–7377–0957–X (hardback : alk. paper)
l. California—Gold discoveries—Juvenile literature. 2. California—History—1846–1850—Juvenile literature. 3. Frontier and pioneer life—California—Juvenile literature. [1. California—Gold discoveries. 2. California—History—1846–1850. 3. Frontier and pioneer life—California.] I. Kallen, Stuart A., 1955– II. Title. III. Series.
F865 .B6525 2002
979.4'04—dc21

2001005780

10911 Technology Place, San Diego, CA 92127

Printed in the U.S.A.

Contents

Chapter One

Rushing to California

On January 23, 1848, a small group of workers at Sutter's Mill on the American River were building a sawmill to cut up logs. When the job was finished, the men flooded river water into a channel under the mill wheel to turn the giant saw blade. By the next morning, the American River had washed away the sand and gravel under the wheel, and a shiny golden nugget appeared under the water.

Workers at the mill soon found more gold nuggets and used them to buy products at a trading post in nearby Sutterville. In May, Sam Brannan, one of the owners of the trading post, went to the mill and found some gold himself. Brannan did not plan to become a miner. Instead, he bought up all the mining supplies he could find and put them up for sale in his trading post. Brannan planned to make a fortune the easy way—by selling supplies to miners.

The workers at Sutter's Mill never imagined that a small piece of gold, about half the size of a pea, would unleash a fever for riches that would bring a quarter of a million people rushing to California from all over the world.

Gold was first discovered in California at Sutter's Mill.

Spreading the Word

To advertise his business, Sam Brannan traveled about one hundred miles to San Francisco where he walked up and down the streets carrying a bottle of gold he had found at Sutter's Mill. Brannan shouted to anyone who would listen that gold could be found in the American River.

Some of the San Franciscans who saw Brannan's gold traveled to the area around Sutter's Mill. A few lucky miners returned to San Francisco as rich men, carrying small sacks of gold. By summertime, the number of miners around Sutter's Mill increased from a few hundred to four thousand.

Sam Brannan made his money by selling supplies to miners.

California's first newspaper, the *San Francisco Star,* ran stories about the few men who had become rich from finding gold at Sutter's Mill. Before long, gold fever had hit San Francisco and nearly everybody in town left their jobs in search of gold. Businesses and houses were simply left empty as their owners ran off to the goldfields. San Francisco's only school closed, and the one teacher who worked there took his students to find gold along the American River.

Other newspapers got wind of the story, and the rush for riches spread down the California coastline. In San Diego, Los Angeles, Sonoma, and other towns, farm fields were left half-planted and houses were left half-built. Teachers, soldiers, sailors, and priests left their posts. Some California towns were left completely deserted when everybody left to strike it rich. Within months the area around Sutter's Fort was swarming with ten thousand miners from all over California.

Rushing to California

Gold fever spread East across the American continent through letters and newspaper stories about the successes of a few California miners. Convinced they too

San Francisco offered Sam Brannan many new customers.

could become rich, people borrowed money and sold their belongings to pay for the trip to California.

The tens of thousands of men who left their families were called "forty-niners." The name was given to miners who struck out for California in 1849, the peak year of the gold rush.

By fall of 1849, the news had spread across the globe. Cities and towns in South America, China, Europe, and elsewhere were stricken with gold fever. People who lived in war-torn or poverty-stricken countries imagined finding easy money in the golden hills of California.

The Long Ocean Voyage

On the East Coast of the United States many ships that once held trade goods were outfitted to carry forty-niners to California. The long ocean voyage took the gold seekers south to Panama. Once there, the travelers hired natives in dugout canoes to take them across the Panamanian landmass on rivers filled with crocodiles and swarming with mosquitoes.

At the river's end, travelers rode west on mules or horses through hot jungles and towering mountains. On the West Coast of the country, they waited to catch another ship north to San Francisco. Sometimes these ships were delayed for months by bad weather. Some people were stranded in Panama when they ran out of money. Countless numbers died from diseases in the jungle.

Others shunned the trek across Panama and made a thirteen-thousand-mile, twelve-month trip from New

People from around the world traveled by ship to seek their fortunes in California.

York to California by boat. They sailed down to Cape Horn at the southernmost tip of South America, and up the western edge of the Americas to San Francisco.

Whatever route the forty-niners chose, they would have to spend months traveling on stormy and dangerous seas in rickety boats. They weathered strong winds, rain, sleet, and hail. Some people were stranded or killed on broken-down ships which had been hastily repaired to meet the huge demand.

Those who could afford it traveled in style, enjoying concerts and good food on comfortable ships. But for the average traveler, the food on most ships was terrible and often spoiled during the long voyage. Despite the hardships, many travelers survived the journey. By the end of 1849, more than forty thousand people had come to California on about seven hundred ships.

The Overland Rush

For those who traveled to California by sea, the journey took more than a year and was very expensive. The average gold seeker preferred to walk the two-thousand-mile route from St. Louis to Sacramento—a journey that could be completed in four to six months.

The most popular route west was the Oregon Trail that ran from Independence, Missouri, to Portland, Oregon. Those heading to California to seek gold followed the California Trail from southern Idaho, over the Sierra Nevada Mountains in California.

Before the gold rush, only 5,000 had ever made the journey to Sacramento on those trails. In 1849, after

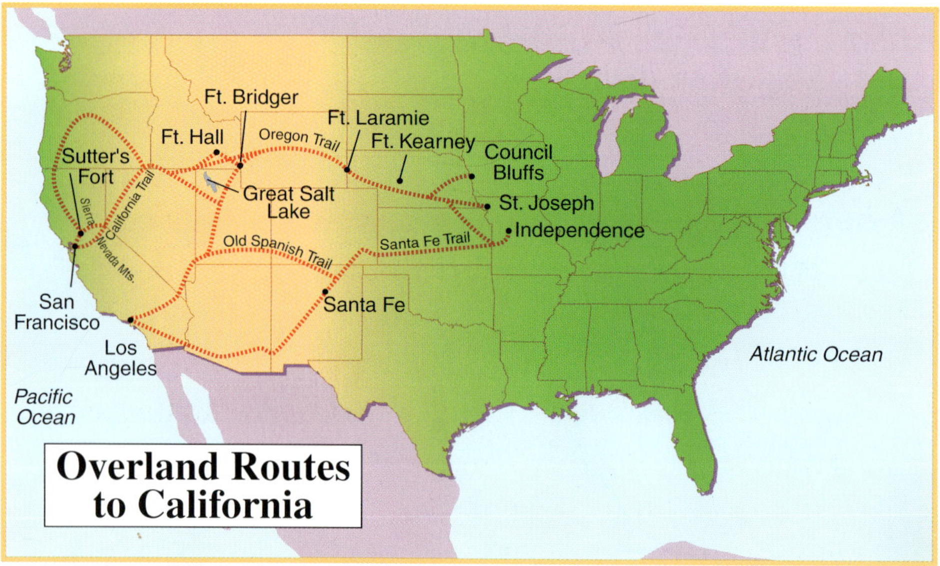

Overland Routes to California

Eager miners travel by wagon train from the eastern part of the United States.

the gold discovery, 30,000 made the trip. In 1850, that number had grown to 50,000 emigrants. And before the gold rush ended in the late 1850s, over 200,000 people had walked to California on those trails.

The first part of the journey involved traveling by stagecoach or steamboat to a major supply station in St. Louis, Missouri. There, the gold seekers bought horses, oxen, flour, bacon, beans, coffee, salt, bedding, tents, tools, ropes, milk cows, chickens, candles, pots, pans, and other supplies.

After the journey began, they restocked food and water supplies at way stations set up along the way. At the way stations, pioneers could join mining companies or other groups that banded together to help one another on the rough journey.

The first part of the trip was exciting and fun for most. Supplies and animals were fresh and the sights were new and interesting. People played music, danced, and rested at night.

Temporary towns sprang up when bad weather or other hardships forced forty-niners to stay in one place for a while. Little towns formed near deep rivers, landslides, and steep mountain passes that were difficult to cross.

Hardships of Travel

The trails crossed many rivers, and these could be deadly to pioneers. Hundreds of people drowned crossing the Kansas, North Platte, and Green Rivers.

Rivers and watering holes were the only sources of drinking water for the travelers, and these became increasingly polluted with human and animal waste. People who drank the water got a deadly disease called cholera which could kill a person in a few hours. With no time or energy to tend to the sick, the pioneers had to leave the dead or dying lying in their beds along the trail. Trails were also littered with dead animals that had died of thirst, hunger, illness, and exhaustion.

The Sierra Nevada Mountains stood in the way of many who tried to reach gold country.

The steep climb over the Sierra Nevada Mountains in eastern California made up the last part of the journey. This was the most difficult part of the trip, and long lines of men, mules, and wagons backed up along the narrow California Trail. Some travelers simply abandoned their wagons, cutting them in half or burning them for fuel, and packing their remaining possessions on the backs of their animals for the rocky climb over the towering mountains.

Western Migration

The discovery of gold in California set off a wave of western migration that continued throughout the nineteenth century. While very few forty-niners actually got rich, fewer still were willing to leave California's warm climate, fertile soil, and natural beauty after their gold-hunting efforts failed. Many went on to start farms and businesses and send for family. From the time of the gold rush, the population of California continued to grow ever larger—and continues to grow even to this very day.

Chapter Two

Life in a Mining Camp

After gold was discovered in California, prospectors came to the state on horses and donkeys, in wagons, coaches, ships, and even on foot. The beautiful hills of northern California suddenly sprouted hundreds of mining camps with colorful names like Bedbug, Git Up and Git, Hangtown, Hell's Delight, Chucklehead Diggings, Squabbletown, Humbug, You Bet, Poker Flats, Poverty Flat, Gouge Eye, and Whiskeytown.

The camps were filled with scruffy, bearded miners with long dirty hair who lived in grubby tents and shacks surrounded by garbage. Like the camps, the miners themselves adopted colorful names such as Fuzzy, Sailor Jack, Hatchet, Frippery Jim, or Hell-Roaring Jo.

Life at the Diggings

The miners called the mountain areas where they dug for gold "the diggings." Gold at the diggings was dug out of the rocky soil beneath rivers and streams. Miners pitched tents or built rough cabins out of logs or bark on the hillsides along the rivers. As rivers became

Mining camps with names like Humbug and Poker Flats sprang up all over northern California.

overcrowded, miners set up camp along dry riverbeds, which they flooded using miles of pipelines.

Men of all nations and colors—and from every walk of life—came together to perform the hard physical labor of mining. Some men worked together in pairs or groups, dividing the labor and sharing expenses. Doctors, lawyers, and politicians worked alongside sailors, farmers, and blacksmiths. They relied on each other in times of illness and injury and worked together to haul wood and cook meals.

Arguments over mining **claims** were common. At some camps, men held meetings to talk about their disagreements and make rules for the group. But as more people crowded into the camps, fists, guns, and knives became the most common methods for solving quarrels.

Food for Miners

Food prices were very high at the camps—and climbed higher as the population grew and demand increased. Flour sold for $800 a barrel, sugar $400. Eggs were $3 apiece and a pound of bread cost $2. This was at a time when a skilled worker made about $2 a day.

High prices were caused by the long distance supplies had to travel before they reached the miners. Food first had to be shipped from agricultural regions to San Francisco, then carted upriver in boats, and finally hauled into large mining camps by horse-drawn wagons. Anything that was left over was then hauled by mules over rough trails to the small mining camps.

The mule trains were usually driven by Mexican men called drovers who tied bells to the animals' bridles. When the miners heard the jingle of mules coming over the steep mountains, they dropped everything and ran toward the suppliers. The mule trains brought food, tools, supplies, and news from home. The desperate miners paid outrageous prices for letters and even newspapers that were six months old.

Fresh meat and vegetables spoiled easily, so they were rarely seen in mining camps. Most miners relied on canned meat, pickled fish, dried beef, dried beans, split peas, and dried fruits such as raisins and figs. These foods kept for long periods of time, along with lard, sugar, molasses, wheat flour, cornmeal, barley, and rice. Miners might also catch fresh fish if they could find still waters undisturbed by another miner. Some hunted near the camps for quail, rabbits, raccoons, or antelope to roast over a fire.

But most miners survived on a diet of greasy meat and salty pickles. Because of their poor nutrition, some became very ill. The most common problem was scurvy, a disease caused by a lack of vitamin C, a nutrient found in fresh fruits and vegetables. Although some doctors lived around the mines, they did not know that scurvy could be cured by eating oranges, lemons, or limes.

Panning for Gold

Very early in the gold rush, gold could be found close to the surface of the riverbeds. This was called **placer** gold,

People came from all over the world in search of gold.

and could be removed by sifting through the sand in the rivers.

The simplest way to remove placer gold was by a method known as **panning.** Miners began by digging up a quantity of what they hoped was gold-bearing sand. Dumping the mixture into Indian baskets, tin cups, old hats, blankets, or heavy metal pans, the miners added a steady stream of water to wash out the dirt. Gold, being heavier, sank to the bottom. Panning required patience, skill, and much physical labor. Miners had to stoop or squat at the river's edge, constantly shaking or rotating their pans.

Placer miners often had to shovel more than two thousand pounds of sand, silt, and gravel everyday

Miners pan for gold in a California river.

just to find enough gold to pay for their food. Thousands of men worked extremely hard but could not even make enough money to survive in the camps. Some miners panned and panned but found nothing at all. A few lucky people struck it rich in a very short time, inspiring others to continue at their difficult task.

When miners found **pay dirt** in a particular place, they **staked** a claim by driving stakes into the ground to mark their spot. If the miner did not use the site for a week, however, he could lose his claim, unless he was ill. If an argument broke out over who owned a claim, another miner or group of miners would help settle the argument.

Weak from poor nutrition, sunburned, and sore, the miners worked with heavy tools while standing hip-deep in freezing water and mud. They suffered from fever, fatigue, aching backs, poison oak, and insect bites. Working day in and day out, their feet and hands became numb, swollen, smashed, and rubbed raw.

Entertainment

Miners worked hard from sunup to sundown, but when night came, they knew how to have a good time. Some miners sang and played music on banjos, fiddles, or guitars. There were few women in the mining camps, so men had to dance with each other. Occasionally miners paid Chinese acrobats or jugglers from San Francisco to travel to their towns to perform.

The men also liked to get together to tell tall tales and cheat at cards. Miners held contests such as boxing, wrestling, horse races, cockfights, dogfights, bullfights, and fights between bulls and bears. Whenever there was a competition, miners were willing to bet their hard-won gold on the outcome. Above all, gambling and drinking were the main forms of entertainment.

Although some miners worked seven days a week just to buy their ration of meat, most rested from their work on Sundays. Some washed and mended their best shirts to dress up and go to church meetings held in tents. Others wrote letters, read books, baked bread, or mended tools.

Chapter Three

Life in a Boom Town

California's population grew quickly as miners flooded in. New towns and cities sprouted up practically overnight in wilderness areas where bears, coyotes, and wolves still roamed.

Many of these **boom** towns grew up around stores that sold food and mining supplies. Sacramento, for instance, was built up around the store of Sam Brannan, who helped start the rush by announcing the gold discovery in San Francisco. By the 1850s, thousands of people had moved to Sacramento, a few miles from Sutter's Fort.

Other suppliers followed Brannan's lead, many of them ex-miners themselves. Some of these traders bought tools and goods at low prices from failed miners who were going back home. These items were quickly resold at much higher prices to newcomers who were called **greenhorns**.

Merchants made huge profits selling shovels, tools, cookware, and clothing. Bakers, blacksmiths, doctors, grocers, pharmacists, saddle makers, and shoemakers also set up shops nearby. Hotels, saloons, restaurants, and gambling houses made fortunes from lonely miners looking for entertainment.

Saloons provided a great source of entertainment for miners.

One of the most successful merchants was Levi Strauss, who came to California with heavy canvas to make tents for the miners. When he met a miner who needed a sturdy pair of pants, he made some out of scraps of the canvas. Other miners soon demanded Levi's tough denim pants, and Levi Strauss started a clothing empire in San Francisco.

San Francisco

Few towns in history have ever experienced the rapid growth that San Francisco did during the gold rush. Before 1848, only two ships a year visited the sleepy little town, which housed about eight hundred people. In 1849, however, over thirty-two thousand people flooded into San Francisco on more than a thousand ships.

Many different languages could be heard on the streets including Chinese, English, French, German, Italian, Portuguese, Spanish, and Swedish.

With so many new people in the little city, housing was very scarce. But San Francisco harbor was cluttered with hundreds of abandoned ships whose sailors had run off in search of gold. People took advantage of the situation, turning the ships into homes, hotels, restaurants, or warehouses. They even built miles of crude wooden bridges so they could walk between the floating shelters.

No part of the ships went to waste. The old sails were made into tents, and a large tent city was hastily built on San Francisco's now-famous Telegraph Hill.

City of Men

The most profitable businesses in San Francisco were saloons. By the end of 1849, the city had five hundred saloons and forty-six gambling houses. The saloons lit up the streets well into the night, and all kinds of music could be heard, along with the sounds of rowdy drunken arguments, gunfire, and breaking glass.

The city had no hospitals or police stations to help people and with no police, crime was rampant, and roving street gangs terrorized the town.

There were few women in this wild boom town. In fact, about 98 percent of San Francisco's population was made up of men. Politicians felt that the presence of more women would help to settle the restless society. Women were invited from all parts of the world to come to the region, and in the last six months of 1849, about five hundred women arrived in the booming city.

Once sleepy San Francisco grew rapidly when gold fever hit.

Women and Business

Many of the women earned very good wages from baking, cooking, sewing, and doing laundry for the gold miners. Nancy Gooch is a good example. Gooch came to the gold mines as an African American slave in 1849, but was freed when California became a state in 1850. She worked as a cook, washerwoman, and seamstress and earned enough money to buy the freedom of her enslaved son and his wife in Missouri. After her son moved to California, he earned enough money to buy Sutter's Mill, the site where gold was first found.

Luzena Wilson was another woman who did very well during the gold rush. Soon after arriving at the goldfields, Wilson was cooking biscuits over a fire to feed her family. Other miners came by to ask if she would sell some of her bread to them. She began cooking for the miners, and soon made enough money to buy herself a profitable hotel.

Wilson's hotel, and most others in the city, offered home-cooked meals for the miners. But the prices were much higher than anywhere else in America because newly rich miners were eager to show off their money. Gold rush restaurants offered lavish meals with high quality ingredients. They competed to offer the finest menus, along with a large selection of wines and cigars.

Hotels also offered a wide variety of entertainment. South American women performed the popular fandango dance to the applause of audiences. There were candles for footlights, and miners threw nuggets of gold to the women onstage.

Singers, comedians, and actors performed on stages or even on pool tables pushed together. In larger mining towns, tents were set up and used as theaters for traveling entertainers. Actors performed in dramas and in comedies about the mining experience. Traveling musicians played folk music from faraway countries to cheer up homesick miners.

But the dance halls and saloons were also dangerous places, filled with tobacco smoke and drunk, unruly men. After working hard all week, miners might start drinking on a Saturday night and not stop until Monday morning. Rowdy behavior was so common that mining towns passed laws against swearing and fighting in front of women and children.

Working Children

Life during the gold rush was especially difficult for children who lived in the boom towns. There were very few schools and most miners lived in tents in the wilderness. Despite the dangers, children as young as seven or eight worked as miners' helpers by cooking, cleaning tools, and sifting through sand in search of gold nuggets.

In larger cities, children worked in hotels, restaurants, or stores. Others were able to earn money working as newsboys. In fact, selling newspapers was a very profitable job for a child. Newsboys often wore fancy clothes and were able to help support their families with the wages they earned.

Hotels hired fandango dancers to entertain miners.

Rowdy behavior was common and saloons were dangerous places.

Some of the children who found their way to the boom towns were orphans who lived in abandoned shanties. These youngsters sometimes belonged to gangs and supported themselves by committing petty crimes.

Young pickpockets and muggers were just one more danger visitors faced in California's gold rush boom towns. In the scramble for riches, the region became a lawless land filled with aggressive young men. It would take several years before the nature of the boom towns would change and law and order would be restored out of the chaos of the gold rush.

Chapter Four

Law and Order

In the early days of the gold rush, there was plenty of land for everybody. But as more people streamed into California, the competition for mining claims increased. Miners began digging on privately owned land that was already settled and fenced in. When no land was left to claim, they **jumped** the claims of other miners. Others sold land that did not belong to them to trusting greenhorns.

In their lust for gold, miners destroyed land, water, homes, buildings, roads, and farms. They killed and ate animals that belonged to farmers and stole crops from the fields. They polluted the water and carved up the landscape with their claims.

As more people flooded in, there was less gold and more violence. In 1849, thousands of experienced criminals, gangsters, and escaped convicts arrived at the goldfields. By 1850, crimes such as robbery, claim jumping, **swindling**, whipping, hanging, lynching, shooting, and mob violence became common events. Miners lived in fear for their lives and their gold.

With no police force, it was up to each miner to guard his own claim from gangs of violent claim jumpers. Miners slept at their work sites with loaded guns under their blankets. In some camps miners formed their own police patrols to watch the claims night and day. Despite these efforts, crime was out of control. It was common to hear lurid tales of roaming gangs of thieves who had robbed or killed miners, store owners, ranchers, and other settlers.

Gangs and Vigilantes

In San Francisco, the two most feared gangs were called the Hounds and the Sydney Ducks. The Hounds

Crime rose as more and more people joined the search for gold.

were former military men who had come from New York. They claimed to want to enforce law and order. Instead, they threatened store owners in order to get free food, drink, and other goods. When they were not given what they wanted, they destroyed and looted businesses. Through bribes and threats, these men practically controlled the city government.

The Sydney Ducks from Australia were escaped convicts. They wore red shirts and caps, and carried knives in their greasy leather belts. The Ducks started fires, then looted during the confusion and panic they caused. They also waited for miners to come into town with sacks of gold, then murdered them in dark alleys.

Citizens of San Francisco formed a citizens' group in 1849 to bring these gangs to justice. The group, called the Vigilance Committee, had up to eight thousand members and was led by Sam Brannan.

The **Vigilantes**, as they were called, became a violent mob themselves. They were armed men who defied city government and publicly executed criminals. Under the **vigilance** of the Vigilantes, the Hounds and the Ducks quickly ceased to exist.

Frontier Justice

The Vigilantes were necessary because very few sheriffs, mayors, judges, or other officers of the law existed. In some regions, private citizens or army officers set up local governments to maintain law and order. Other areas had no government at all. In isolated mining

Vigilantes used violence to fight crime.

camps and towns, people developed their own sets of rules, called "frontier justice," for resolving problems.

When somebody was suspected of a crime, frontier justice was served up in "miners' courts." At a trial, short speeches were given for and against the suspect. In smaller camps, miners acted as judge and jury,

People who lived in areas with no government sometimes resolved problems in their own way.

deciding who was guilty and what punishment they would receive. Since these courts varied greatly, the same crime might have a very different punishment from place to place.

In some larger mining towns, courts were set up and judges were appointed. While some judges had studied the law and were honest, others were dishonest and trying to get rich. In San Francisco in 1849, a street-corner peanut seller was allowed to become a judge. He ordered everyone who appeared before him to pay a bribe of one ounce of gold. This judge did not listen to speeches about guilt and innocence, or appoint a jury to hear them. He simply made his decision based on bribes, then moved along to the next case.

Racism

The groups who experienced the most injustice during the gold rush were the Native Americans, Asians, Mexicans, and other ethnic groups who lived in California.

The Chinese were made fun of and bullied because their appearance and habits set them apart from others. They were also easy to rob and kill, since they rarely carried guns.

Even though Native Americans and Latinos had lived in California before the European-Americans arrived, they were insulted, bullied, and subjected to racism. Mexicans, Chileans, French, and East Indians also experienced racism. Prejudice was often used as a way to justify stealing gold and jumping claims. As more and more people poured into the goldfields, law and order quickly disappeared leading to a state of gang warfare.

Law and order came slowly to California after it became a state on September 9, 1850. With statehood, thousands of white American men poured into the goldfields of California. These men succeeded in getting laws passed requiring "foreign" miners to pay a monthly license fee. More than ten thousand Mexican miners were forced to give up their claims and return to Mexico.

Mexicans and Native Americans, who had lived in the area before it became a state, were included in the list of foreigners who did not have the same rights as white male citizens of the United States.

Because of the bias favoring white people in the courts, crimes committed by American men were sometimes tolerated. There were cases of white miners beating, attacking, murdering, and lynching miners from other groups, especially Chinese and Mexican people.

But none suffered more than the Native Americans who lived near the goldfields. Miners attacked their villages, destroyed crops, burned their homes, and murdered entire families.

The End of the Boom

The great California gold rush lasted a few short years. By 1853, over one hundred thousand forty-niners had swarmed across the countryside, and nearly every stream in the central part of the state had been scoured for gold. That year, over $67 million was taken from the goldfields—an incredible sum at the time. The big bonanza, however, was coming to an end. The easy-to-reach placer gold was exhausted and miners were forced to look through dirt piles left behind by earlier prospectors.

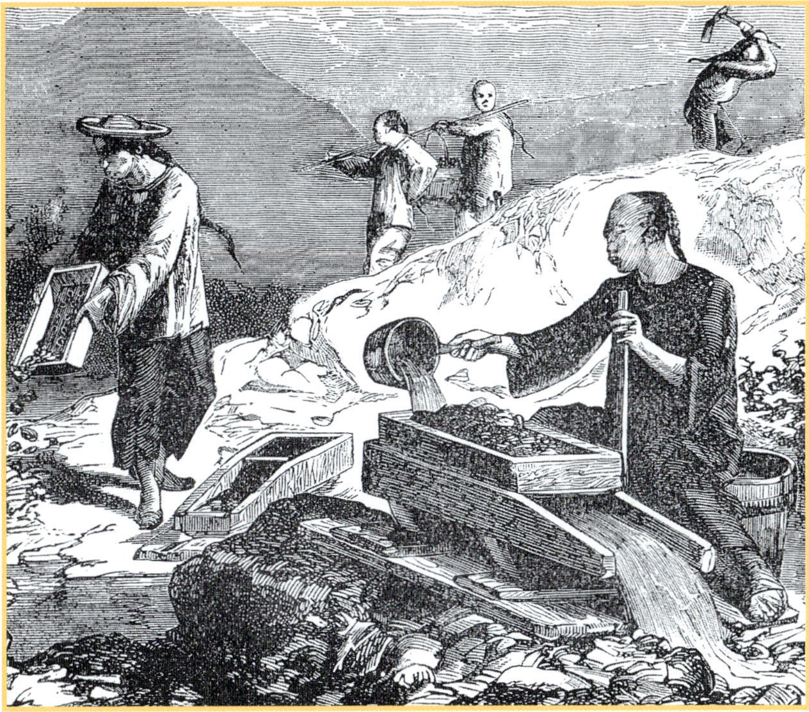

Chinese miners suffered abuse because of their appearance and customs.

For the next twenty-five years, nearly a billion dollars worth of gold would be taken from California. This wealth would help make the United States one of the richest countries in the world. The gold was still in the hills, but complicated machinery and college-educated engineers took the place of the miner with his mule and his pan.

Most miners left to seek other riches—a gold rush broke out in Colorado in 1859. During the six years of the California gold rush, over 250,000 people had moved to the state where only 14,000 immigrants had

No one could have predicted the wealth that lay in the northern California countryside.

lived before. San Francisco had grown overnight from a quiet town full of whaling boats and schooners to a major center of finance. Men who struck it rich during the gold rush took center stage in world politics, agriculture, and manufacturing.

California was changed forever by the gold rush. By 1860, 380,000 people had moved to the Golden State. On a gamble or a dare, a huge migration of diverse people came together for a great adventure. They were hoping to get rich, and they created a prosperous new state instead.

Glossary

boom: to grow quickly

claim: public land staked out by a miner

greenhorn: a newcomer who is easily fooled

jump: to seize or occupy illegally

panning: using a pan to separate gold from gravel by washing with water

pay dirt: earth that is profitable to mine

placer: sand or gravel that contains valuable minerals, such as gold

stake: to claim as one's own by marking the location with stakes

swindle: to cheat out of money or property

vigilance: alert watchfulness

Vigilante: one who believes in taking the law into one's own hands

For Further Exploration

Arthur Blake and Pamela Dailey, *The Gold Rush of 1849: Staking a Claim in California.* Brookfield, CT: Millbrook Press, 1995. The story of the California gold rush and its effect on the history of the United States.

Stephen Krensky, *Striking It Rich: The Story of the California Gold Rush.* New York: Simon & Schuster, 1996. Describes the discovery of gold in California and its impact on the development of California and the West.

A. I. Lake, *Gold Fever.* Vero Beach, FL: Rourke, 1990. Describes the origins of the California gold rush that began in 1848, the individuals and mining techniques involved, and the resulting wealth, destruction, and tragedy.

Jim Rawls, *Dame Shirley and the Gold Rush.* New York: Raintree Steck-Vaughn, 1993. Relates how a series of letters, written by a woman known as Dame Shirley and published in a San Francisco magazine in 1854 and 1855, helped to relate the true story of the California gold rush.

Rosalyn Schanzer, *Gold Fever! Tales from the California Gold Rush.* Washington, DC: National Geographic Society, 1999. Uses lighthearted illustrations and excerpts from letters, journals, and newpaper articles to relate the story of the California gold rush of 1848.

R. Conrad Stein, *The Story of the Gold at Sutter's Mill.* Chicago: Childrens Press, 1981. Presents the scene in California after gold was discovered at John Sutter's sawmill and the subsequent fortunes made and lost.

Index

Picture Credits

Cover: Bridgeman Art Library International Ltd.
© Archivo Iconografico, S.A./CORBIS, 28
© Bettmann/CORBIS, 39, 40
Colorado Historical Society, 19
© CORBIS, 7
© Hulton/Archive by Getty Images, 16, 33
Chris Jouan, 10
© North Wind Picture Archives, 5, 6, 9, 20, 24, 30, 35, 36
© Réunion des Musées Nationaux/Art Resource, 26
© Scala/Art Resource, 11
© Brian Vikander/CORBIS, 13

About the Authors

P. M. Boekhoff is a professional artist who has illustrated many book covers and cowritten several children's books on the subjects of art, ecology, and Native Americans. In her spare time Ms. Boekhoff creates large paintings, writes poetry, studies herbal medicine, and tends her garden.

Stuart A. Kallen is the author of more than 150 nonfiction books for children and young adults. He has written extensively about Native Americans and American history. In addition, Mr. Kallen has written award-winning children's videos and television scripts. In his spare time, Stuart A. Kallen is a singer/songwriter/guitarist in San Diego, California.